WEEP BEFORE GOD

Books by John Wain

Poetry
A WORD CARVED ON A SILL

Fiction
HURRY ON DOWN
LIVING IN THE PRESENT
THE CONTENDERS
A TRAVELLING WOMAN
NUNCLE AND OTHER STORIES
STRIKE THE FATHER DEAD

Criticism
PRELIMINARY ESSAYS

WEEP
BEFORE GOD

Poems
by John Wain

LONDON

MACMILLAN & CO LTD

NEW YORK · ST MARTIN'S PRESS

1962

MACMILLAN AND COMPANY LIMITED
London Bombay Calcutta Madras Melbourne

THE MACMILLAN COMPANY OF CANADA LIMITED
Toronto

ST MARTIN'S PRESS INC
New York

PRINTED IN GREAT BRITAIN

Weep before God, laugh before men.

—Jewish proverb

NEVILL'S

CONTENTS

Time Was

EIRIAN'S

A MIND ago I took the stones for clay
And thought a man could foot it like a beast;
But animals have no hard words to say.
We too were shielded once, but that has ceased.
A daisy gleams as coldly as a star,
And flints are hard because I know they are.

Time was I watched the minnows in the brook.
I took them for my brothers and my wives,
Till I bent closer for a second look
And saw that they were swimming for their lives.
Survival was their magic and their art:
How could I bear their coldness near my heart?

I knew I was not animal or plant.
My way was harder: I could read the signs.
But still my blood drowned sermons with its chant;
My bones were hard as rock, yet soft as vines.
Blood, time and judgment whipped me into fear:
I trembled at the ticking in my ear.

Time was I thought the dead lay down to rest
As snug as shiny pebbles in the earth,
Their stories ended and their bones undressed.
I knew that pebbles had no second birth.
Tonight my breath acknowledges its hosts—
The living man is cradled by his ghosts.

We need not envy what the ghosts can do.
We shall be filmy spirits in our turn.
Let me rejoice to punch a window through
And gash my fist, touch flame and feel it burn!
When I'm a ghost, I'll caper through a wall.
I'll loll at ease beneath a waterfall.

Time was I thought that ghosts were tame as hens
And flew no higher than a man could leap,
And that when death had smashed the spirit's lens
The lonely body cried itself to sleep.
Not mind but marrow set my error right.
My veins grew round like saplings to the light.

I wonder now why I was born dismayed.
What was the shape that gibbered through the room?
Who told me that all good men were afraid?
I think I lay and trembled in the womb,
As mindlessly as rags flap in the wind.
My soul knew guilt before my body sinned.

To live is to go forward and forget.
My shattered bones knit up and march again.
I paid for all mistakes with drops of sweat
Strained from the reasty gammon of my pain.
Now that I start my journey to the truth,
Let me set down the burdens of my youth!

I know the earth has strength to make me strong:
Its patient sinews stretch from pole to pole.
Beasts, men and minerals know right from wrong—
O hear the timber groaning into coal!
I cupped my eyes: nine seasons I lay prone:
Now, looking up, I find the world has grown.

Time was I thought the world was thin and dry,
A heap of shavings curled from heaven's blade.
(Let fall a match, the flames would hit the sky.)
I tried to hide, but shavings give no shade.
The sunlight pierced my vitals like a knife.
I writhed: I opened: suffering was life.

A wind kissed leaf and lake: that wind was I;
At last the desert flowered with delight.
I heard the stars drum in the hollow sky.
Roused by that drumming, here I stand upright.
Now let my fossils lie: no more retreat:
My hopes are sharp as glass before my feet!

Poem Without a Main Verb

WATCHING oneself
being clever, being clever:
keeping the keen equipose between *always* and *never*;

delicately divining
(the gambler's sick art)
which of the strands must hold, and which may part;

playing off, playing off
with pointless cunning
the risk of remaining against the risk of running;

balancing, balancing
(alert and knowing)
the carelessly hidden with the carefully left showing;

endlessly, endlessly
finely elaborating
the filigree threads in the web and the bars in the grating;

at last minutely
and thoroughly lost
in the delta where profit fans into cost;

with superb navigation
afloat on that darkening, deepening sea,
helplessly, helplessly.

This Above All is Precious and Remarkable

THIS above all is precious and remarkable,
How we put ourselves in one another's care,
How in spite of everything we trust each other.

Fishermen at whatever point they are dipping and lifting
On the dark green swell they partly think of as home
Hear the gale warnings that fly to them like gulls.

The scientists study the weather for love of studying it,
And not specially for love of the fishermen,
And the wireless engineers do the transmission for love of
    wireless,

But how it adds up is that when the terrible white malice
Of the waves high as cliffs is let loose to seek a victim,
The fishermen are somewhere else and so not drowned.

And why should this chain of miracles be easier to believe
Than that my darling should come to me as naturally
As she trusts a restaurant not to poison her?

They are simply examples of well-known types of miracle,
The two of them,
That can happen at any time of the day or night.

Distances To Go

YES, when you die, so much depends
on how long a journey it involves
as particle to particle descends.

I've known people prefer, like wolves,
to lope with bellies almost touching the earth.
(it makes them feel insecure, the way it revolves.)

And too high fliers disintegrate, falling. It's not worth
bothering where their grains meet the ground,
they seem to be saying; as if air, not mud, gave birth

to their rare natures. Some, by contrast, are found
hanging in attics or otherwise not caring why,
how, or through what arc of sky they were downed.

The ones I like best come spiralling from high
up, all right, but in no wise blurringly far from
the tussocky staid earth where, calmly, they look to lie.

Anniversary

THESE are my thoughts on realizing
That I am the same age as my father was
On the day I was born.

As a little scarlet howling mammal,
Crumpled and unformed, I depended entirely on someone
Not very different from what I am to-day.

When I think this over,
I feel more crumpled and unformed than ever:
I ask myself what I have done to compare with *that*.

It also makes me aware, inescapably,
Of having entered upon the high table-land,
The broad flat life of a mature man.

Where everything is seen from its actual distance,
E.g. childhood not so remote as to seem a boring myth,
Nor senility as something that awaits other people.

But deeper than that,
It is like entering a dark cone,
The shadow thrown across my life by the life it derives from.

And deeper than that still,
It is the knowledge that life is the one communicable thing.
It called. I heard it from where I slept in seed and liquid.

The patterns of seed and brine coalesced in a solemn dance,
Whence my life arose in the form of a crest,
And has carried itself blindly forward until now.

In ignorance of its uniqueness until now,
Until I stumbled over these thoughts solid as bricks,
And like bricks fearsome in their everyday squareness.

The New Sun

THE new sun rises in the year's elevation,
Over the low roof's perspective.

It reveals the roughness of winter skin
And the dinginess of winter clothes.

It draws, with a hard forefinger,
a line under the old ways.

Finis! the old ways have become obsolete,
The old skin, the old clothes.

This same sun, like a severe comet,
rises over old disappointments.

It makes us cry out in agony,
this peeling away of old sorrows.

When the sun foretells the death of an old sorrow,
the heart prophetically feels itself an orphan;

a little snivelling orphan, and the sun
its hard-hearted parish officer.

Dear gods, help us to bear the new sun!
Let our firm hearts pray to be orphaned!

Apology for Understatement

FORGIVE me that I pitch your praise too low.
Such reticence my reverence demands,
For silence falls with laying on of hands.

Forgive me that my words come thin and slow.
This could not be a time for eloquence,
For silence falls with healing of the sense.

We only utter what we lightly know.
And it is rather that my love knows me.
It is that your perfection set me free.

Verse is dressed up that has nowhere to go.
You took away my glibness with my fear.
Forgive me that I stand in silence here.

It is not words could pay you what I owe.

On Being Insulted by a Popular Journalist

So this is how it stands: a lout
Can hawk, and gather up his phlegm
And, grinning, spit it in my face
As I walk by; and all without
The fear of censure or disgrace.
His friends see nothing to condemn,
His enemies avert their eyes,
His masters would approve the deed.

Did I foresee when I began
The air so filled with rancorous cries,
The granite that rejects the seed,
The spite of every ignorant man?
But patience: those who climb the path
To where those fruits and flowers grow
Which I have travelled far to seek
May never halt or swerve for wrath:
No, let it be a boast to show
His spittle hanging from my cheek!

To a Friend in Trouble

ON those sharp edges of your broken love
You cut your veins, which do not leak out blood,
But suck in trouble, trouble, to your heart:
What can I say? except that all about us
I see a time of melting, a time of unloosing;
And on my own life's flat horizon, also,
The clouds swim up.
So many faiths dry up or slide away,
So many lovers I see with averted faces
Who wander, and will not stay to be pacified.
Now all our hearts, I think,
Suck in this scalding drug through broken veins,
This dry, ammoniac, destructive pain.
I do not know what I should say to you:
It is the madness of summer beats us down,
The red-eyed sunshine and the pelting rain.
I stand beside you empty of all comfort,
Except to say that now your love is smashed
And gashes at your veins, I feel your pain:
And in these throbbing nights I also see
Those broken edges in my doubtful dreams.

Au Jardin des Plantes

THE gorilla lay on his back,
On hand cupped under his head,
Like a man.

Like a labouring man tired with work,
A strong man with his strength burnt away
In the toil of earning a living.

Only of course he was not tired out with work,
Merely with boredom; his terrible strength
All burnt away by prodigal idleness.

A thousand days, and then a thousand days,
Idleness licked away his beautiful strength,
He having no need to earn a living.

It was all laid on, free of charge.
We maintained him, not for doing anything,
But for being what he was.

And so that Sunday morning he lay on his back,
Like a man, like a worn-out man,
One hand cupped under his terrible hard head.

Like a man, like a man,
One of those we maintain, not for doing anything,
But for being what they are.

A thousand days, and then a thousand days,
With everything laid on, free of charge,
They cup their heads in prodigal idleness.

On the Death of a Murderer

'One day Vera showed us a photograph of some local Gestapo men which
had come into her hands. The photograph had been taken when they were
in the country outside Prague for a day's holiday. The young men were
ranged in two rows in their neat uniforms, and they stared out at us with
professionally menacing but unhappy eyes from that recent past now dead.
    '. . . After the relief of Prague these young men were hunted through the
countryside, Vera told us, like wild game, and all of them taken and killed.'

                                                    Edwin Muir, *Autobiography*.

OVER the hill the city lights leap up.
But here in the fields the quiet dusk folds down.
A man lies in a ditch. He listens hard.
His own fast breathing is the biggest sound,
But through it, coming nearer, he hears another:
The voices of his hunters, coming nearer.

They are coming, and he can run no further.

He was born in a Germany thrashing like a fish
On a gravel towpath beating out its life.
As a child, something they called the Blockade
Nearly strangled him with impersonal cold fingers.
Clever doctors saved his life. The Blockade receded.
He hopped in the Berlin streets like a cool sparrow.
His wise friends showed him a quick way to earn
Pocket-money: while English schoolboys chalked
Dirty words and sniggered behind desk-lids,
He learnt the things the words meant; his pockets
Filled up with change and his heart jingled with hate.

Now his hate has jingled in the ears of Europe.
He has taught them to know the refusal of pity.
His life is nearly over; only the darkness
Covers him as his pursuers cry over the fields.
In a moment they will tear him to pieces.

He was sick of the things that went with the dirty words:
Sick of the pocket-money and the windy street.
Then the uniforms came. They said to him: *Be strong.*

When he was fifteen, he had a gun.
He had forgotten the Blockade and the pocket-money,
Except on nights when he could not sleep: his gun
Was a friend, but when they gave him a whip
He loved that better still. *Be strong!* He cried.

The speeches were made, the leaves fell, it was war.
To smashed Prague his gun and his whip led him in time.
There, he learnt the delight of refusing pity.

Did he never wonder about those he murdered?
Never feel curious about the severe light
That flamed in their irises as they lay dying?
Apparently not. His duty took all his care.
He fed his starving heart with cruelty
Till it got sick and died. His masters applauded.
Once, he dragged off a man's lower jaw.

Now they are coming nearer over the fields.
It is like the Blockade, only worse. He will die.
They have taken away his whip and gun.

But let us watch the scene with a true eye.
Arrest your pen, hurrying chronicler.
Do you take this for a simple act: the mere
Crushing of a pest that crawled on the world's hide?
Look again: is there not an ironic light
In the fiery sky that rings his desperate head?

He will die, this cursed man. The first pursuer
Is here. The darkness is ready to give him up.
He has, at most, a hundred breaths to draw.

But what of the cunning devil that jerked his strings?
Is that one idle, now that the strings are cut?

The man's body will rot under lime, and that soon.
But the parades have taught his uniform to march.
The hunters close in: do they feel the danger?
When they wrench his body to pieces, will they hear
A sigh as his spirit is sucked into the air
That they must breathe? And will his uniform
March on, march on, across Europe? Will their children
Hop in the streets like cool sparrows, and draw
His spirit into their hopeful lungs? Will
Their hearts jingle with hate? And who shall save them
If after all the years and all the deaths
They find a world still pitiless, a street
Where no grass of love grows over the hard stones?

Poem

Hippolytus. Do you see my plight, Queen, stricken as I am?
Artemis. I see. But my eyes are not permitted to shed tears.

Euripides, *Hippolytus,* 1395–6.

LIKE a deaf man meshed in his endless silence
the earth goes swishing through the heavens' wideness.

Doubtless some god with benign inquiring brow
could lean over and let his brown eye so true

play over its whirling scabby hide with a look of searching
till suddenly, with eye and bland forefinger converging

he points to a specially found spot. *Here, this moment*
he might say, *I detect it; this is the locus of torment:*

This spot is the saddest on earth's entire crust.
A quaint fancy? Such gods can scarcely exist?

Still, the fact outlives the metaphor it breeds;
whether or not the god exists, the scored earth bleeds.

There must be a point where pain takes its worst hold.
One spot, somewhere, holds the worst grief in the world.

Who would venture a guess as to where this grief lies cupped?
Ah, from minute to minute it could never be mapped.

For trouble flies between molecules like a dream.
It flowers from the snapped edge of bones like sour flame.

Who knows what child lies in a night like a mine-shaft
unblinking, his world like a fallen apple mashed and cleft?

Or what failed saint plummets into his private chasm
having bartered all Heaven for one stifling orgasm?

Or perhaps it is even an animal who suffers worst,
gentle furry bundle or two-headed obscene pest.

But where pain's purest drop burns deep no one could say,
unless it were this god with benign brown eye.

Some would curse this god for doing nothing to help.
But he has knowledge like cold water on his scalp.

To perceive that spirit of suffering in its raging purity
is to a god the burden of his divinity.

O then, if he exists, have pity on this god.
He is clamped to that wounded crust with its slime of blood.

He has no ignorance to hold him separate.
Everything is known to a god. The gods are desperate.

To Be Continued

It was a world without women,
They stalked across, the heroes of our boyhood,
Their shoulders forming the giant shape of courage.
They fought big cats or skidded round banking,
Buried their blades behind the heads of sharks,
Cried to the crocodiles, 'Here comes a man!' then dived.
Through vistas of serials they strode,
Bravely enduring the tattooist's needle,
Taking from foreigners no back-chat:
Fisting through palisades of wops and japs,
Trusting no dago,
Except the crack-shot gaucho.

By the green hedges we hid in their summer shadows.
Their lives were geared to the single shaft of courage:
Our tired fathers, brief-case and Morris,
Were men in a different manner.
We sniffed at the mild fields in their simple drizzle:
No cactus towered in the garden.
Turning the pages, absorbing our patchwork legend,
We bided our time for adventure:
All we needed was inches.

But all the time we were reading,
Our epic world was slowly listing over:
Time sprang a leak and our immunity
Sighed out like gas before we noticed.
Yes, hanging rapt above the dog-eared page
Chewing on dreams of manhood, simmered tender
On formula's gas-ring,
We never raised our eyes to see
The anaconda inching down the trunk,
The cruel Redskin aiming.

At last the Chinese pirates of desire
Rushed in a body: with the captain shot
Dead in the wheel-house, the chart of boyhood lost,
Our gallant tramp hove to:
At the swing of a linen skirt we struck our colours.

This was the real jungle of claw and creeper.
Macaws flashed in the green light, but we knew
No language of signals: tenderfeet all,
We roamed for escape as far as Klondyke and Yukon.
The Mounties always get their man. We were
So lately the Mounties: suddenly, now, the men.

Lurching down forest paths where once we reigned,
We felt, too late, the rotten sticks cave in.
Down we pitched into the ambush-pit of sex.
The yelling natives swarmed with net and pole.
What happened? This used to be our pampas.
In the snows we fared no better. Our base camp
Abandoned, tins of bully fresh till doomsday,
We plummeted down the Everest of the nipple,
Our bobsleigh crashed on the curve of a thigh,
Bounced like a mad thing.

So we abandoned ship, camped on an ice-floe.
Shouting 'mush' we started the long trek:
The walruses bobbed on the water in mockery.
It was all over, and we knew it.
Our tents whisked away in the fifteenth-year blizzard.

Sadly we packed away our heroes.
Good-bye to the stern-jawed men of decision!
Their adventures were too tame,
They who had never bitten the wormy apple.

Now we stood alone facing the mad horns,
Knowing neither flight nor courage would save us,
Neither truth nor lies;
We must go down where sharks wheeled in the gloom,
Do battle with the unfair octopus.

For the press-gang of lust and heartbreak were on us,
And pleasure winked like the deluding sea.
We could sign on as second mate, or snug below decks
Hear the slap of the green waves.
In either case, there was no escaping that terrible hornpipe.

Perhaps, one day,
When the years have rolled in a ragged circle
To where the eggs of motive lie in their nest,
We shall go back to our heroes.
The legionaries will stand for the last parade,
Minor characters dead of cafard and thirst,
Still straining after a mirage of eyelashes,
And the cold bugle will sound.
The survivors will get their passage home,
There, by firelight, to re-enter the land
Of the cool freeman whose silhouette conceals
No awkward bag of honey; be once more
Like him, exempt from the swollen itch of liking,
And only in dreams
Remember the thicket and the misleading passage.

A Handshake for Brave Culture-Uncles

As mice tread round in drums for exercise
Or cage-birds walk up ladders to ring bells,

So you, good hominids, mime Tarzan bold,
Swinging on nylon ropes from tree to tree.

'Big game stampede to safety when we scold!
At every smirk a reputation dies!'

So: thump your chests, and roar. Then home to tea.
How like a window-box this jungle smells!

A Boisterous Poem About Poetry

I HAVE a notion that the world is round.
The headlong sun, forever riding down,
Is always rising on another scene.
The thought is apposite for poets now:
They fell too promptly into step, and marched
Behind the hearse of poetry, which swayed
And rumbled, full of dignity and plumes,
Piled high with wreaths from children, colleagues, friends.
Even the best did this. Such leaden skies,
Such evening wheel of swallows and of bats—
Surely it meant the closing of a life.
Bravely, they sighed farewell: 'The too late born,
Who would have served her long, she predeceased.'
Pity they wasted so much stoic pride!
That funeral will never reach the grave.
Nothing as great as poetry can die:
Not dusk, but dawn sprays colour on the clouds.
Not death, but a prolonged exhausted sleep,
The prologue to renewal and fresh deeds,
Seals down those eyelids.
                              Now the coffin jolts,
The lid flies open, wreaths slide to the ground.
Gather them up! These flowers are for her!
Tear off those labelled words of sympathy:
Strike matches, burn those bands of solemn crepe:
Let funeral cartwheel into festival!

I say this is a time for poetry.
I name today the greatest of all days
That ever called a poet out to sing.

Not for its gentleness, for it has none:
Not for its colour or its love of song,
For it has none of either, as we know.
It is the empty clangour of its need,
Its wilderness of craving silences
That makes me call today a poet's day.
The themes, the themes! The unattempted songs!
The dictionaries crammed with eager ghosts!
Our hearts are ill with silence. Someone must sing:
We have grown yellow on a diet of prose.
I swear I almost find it in my heart
To love the phoneys and the strutting liars
Who bray and belch and rattle on tin cans
And claim that they are singing: trading on
The ignorant ear that never heard true song,
And, baffled, must take noise for music. At least
They make a cheerful noise. I could forgive
Even the worst, the con. men who harangue
Their fellow artists, or the commercial saints.
I pardon even those who pretend to sing:
But those who truly sing, who know the weight
Of cold invisible laurels, and yet stand
Upright, and bless their burden, these I love.
So, no more talk of funerals. Begin!

II

No excuses! There is material everywhere.
Every life has grief, and grief makes poems.
It is easy material, fit for beginners.

No novice is without his bag of despair,
To scatter poem-seeds on the ground,
And water them freely.

But beyond this there is true grief,
The seeds that really do grow,
Not into poems, but into flowers.

The black flower of grief grows in any soil.
Bend down, and gather an armful,
Of your own, or your neighbour's.

It is an easy subject, to start with.
Tears are a good predictable mixture
Like rocks and heather.

And there have never been eyes without tears,
Never once.

III

Then sing the hurt of hate
when the black petals spin down from a cold sky
like poisoned snow.

Can you do anything without someone hating you?
Or feel anything without hating someone?

And hate hurts! So sing the crazy
lyric of the hurt, sing the red cry
of the flesh caught in the curt
rollers of hate, of the skin
brushed by the nettle-petals circling
down from the cold sky! She
hates me, I hate
him, you hate
them, we
HATE
AND
our muscles when
the poison touches them

24

bunch out and jerk our limbs:
we dance and leap, whether we will or no.
So join the dance of hate, and strew the ground
with poisoned petals—the black flower in your teeth,
and the hot drumstick of hate thumping your heart!

IV

But hatred can be ink in a poet's pen.
Come, let us believe in the usefulness of satire!
Whether it does any good or not, let us kick!
Kick the hired liars shouting for sixpences,
The ad. man thumbing his manual of deceptions:
Kick the upright corpse with the rotting face
Who hates his fellow-men from his withered heart,
And wants them all to die and smell like himself:
So he walks among them in a cardboard mask,
To grin for him as he offers his wares.
Kick his tray over, send his pies rolling,
Spill his bright bottles in the common gutter:
Nothing will halt him for long, he has more,
The money flows his way and he flows the money's,
And nothing can fight against such an alliance—
But kick! Kick once, and afterwards be strong,
Endure in silence his leisurely revenge.
Hold up your head, suffer the hail of garbage.
Better than you have walked among it!
And spare a little pity for the sweating money-slaves
Trapped in their bright anxious hell, tattle and gibber.
Think of spending twenty-four hours on the stuff
The shallowest office-girl reads in the bus, then forgets!
Those who take the mail shall perish by the express:
The hand of the gossip-writer is in every man's pocket,
And always leaves the same fat stain behind it.

So kick! Their backsides are padded with banknotes:
A delicious target for the honest toe-cap!

V

Now move closer to the true and difficult centre:
>and sing the mixture.
Braying optimists, number off! Disappear
Into a pearly cloud as fat as Chesterton!
Tuneful pessimists, likewise number off:
Dive into a Shropshire ditch, and farewell.
It is the pain that pricks out the true song,
But the joy that guides the notes to melody.

Think of the origin: think that every policeman,
Every jolly stockbroker in a hired gondola,
Every tall baritone in a philosopher's gown,
All started from the thrashing net of the spawn.
My Lord Bishop was sired in a jingling bed,
Miss Universe seeded in a select motel.

The blind flesh drives cunningly towards renewal.
Our life's starting whistle chirps in this hungry music,
Its first breath yowls in the symphony of discontent—
Two thrusting bipeds locked in a tangle of sheets.

Sing the music—sing the blind aria of the flesh:
Sing the melody pouring from the locked cage.
Allow the hard picture its improving border,
The fascination before, the tenderness afterwards:
But never sentimentalize the blind thrust,
Nor be tempted to blink the harshness,
The clench of antagonism in the fused kiss.
Life is made here, and life is a drawn knot,
A tangle of threads dragged hard as a pebble,
Where amid contraries the lover chews like a cannibal.

VI

Next sing the machine, our glory and disgrace.
Celebrate its possibilities, and tremble
At the cold fury of its many revenges.

It began with metal.
                    Metal hates flesh,
Hates everything that has a beating heart.
The farmer talks to the earth in her own language:
Men who tend beasts walk by the side of the beasts.
But the miner is schooled into rape and violence,
He drags metal from its tucked-in bed of peace,
To be assaulted with fire, to be pressed and stamped,
By its own brothers twisted and tortured.

We make machines from metal, that hates us,
And they are all our enemies in secret.
On the surface they flatter our intelligence,
They are all smiles, they bend to our tasks:
Then suddenly they turn and savage us.
Metal hates flesh!
                    Ask the survivors,
Ask the ragged man with an empty sleeve,
The pale aviator in a wheeled chair.
Come, shape an elegy for victims of the machine!
Hold the world still for long enough
To drop one tear on its own bitter dust!

Machines were born in a dazzle of sunlight,
Fathered by the easy Greek and Italian.
These deft ones fondled metal as a birthday toy.
Its uniformity was a new scale of music.
How fast, with bright chisels for finger-nails,
They would prise off the caked mud of old ways:
How cleanly, with a jaw full of swords,

They would bite through to an aery dimension!

Here speaks the man of the Renaissance,
His head in a cool rainbow of the future,
His private parts kicking in a mad cage.
Strange that he, who understood so much
That his lightest dream glistened with consciousness,
Never heard the vengeful cry of the torn earth
Or the hot curse shouted from the anvil.

But we hear it, we hear it all the time:
The invective of metal rings in our hollow skulls.
Come, your battle-songs! Your slow chants for the fallen!

VII

This is the simple curse of the machine.
But there is also a complicated curse.
Sing next of those whom the machine has tamed
Into its own steel-hearted servitude.
The trap was baited fifty years ago,
When men thought aeroplanes were angels' wings
And that the wireless was the voice of God.
'Men like gods!' cried eager-beaver Wells:
He knew his own mistake before he died.
He should have postulated men like rods,
Like girders, ratchets, valves and coils of wire.
Examine the new man. What do you see?
A robot flashing slogans from its eyes,
Ticking out spools of slogans from its mouth,
With rubber stamps for slogans in its fists.
I am afraid of death in all its forms:
But the slogan is the killer I fear most,
The killer that leaves the body still alive.
See how the slogan-corpses stride among us,

Booming and quacking from the empty head-piece!
Stand clear, avoid them, if you want to live.
For slogans rot the mind that harbours them,
And when your mind is rotted, you will die.
IF YOU SHOULD FIND YOURSELF INFECTED, PLEASE
REMEMBER THAT DELAY IS DANGEROUS.
TREATMENT IS FREE AND CONFIDENTIAL.
                                        Yes,
Call in the poet with his puncturing needle,
His long pragmatical stethoscope, his eye
Versed in the symptoms of the slogan-pox.
He has the drug that can burn language clean,
To make it fit to put into your mouth:
The greatest antiseptic drug of all,
Antibiotic, disinfectant, harsh,
Yet gentle to all rightful skin and flesh.
Where does he find it? Everywhere he goes.
What does it cost him?
                        Nothing. And everything.
What is it called? It has a spread of names.
Concreteness, honesty, the particular.
A slogan is for crowds: it cannot stand
The simple one-at-a-time of a poet's words.
The genuine justifies the genuine:
A false coin dropped on a stone farmhouse floor
Is heard as false: but every coiner knows
This cannot happen on the boardroom carpet.

VIII

The logic-spider spins his net
for little flies that buzz and fret.

He strings his net from twig to twig:
he does not know that trees are big.

He finds the mountain-top too high
to spin his net and catch his fly.

He feeds on flies that cluster where
The valleys cup the gentle air.

The artist woos the bird that sings
beyond the range of insect-wings.

The watchful scientist must sway
in storms that blow the web away.

These leave the spider to his flies:
they are not wise as he is wise.

Where the peaks jab the frozen sky
is the place where systems die.

Where the air blows harsh and pure
the spider's web will not endure.

Truth is fulness, little spider!
Truth has other truths inside her!

The artist and the man of science
in pretty webs put no reliance.

They know the final thirst and hunger:
they need no definition-monger.

Sleep, spider, while the truth rolls by:
these couplets be your lullaby!

IX

But the truth-hunters have no downy lullaby:
They must doze at the wheel, or drop exhausted
For an hour at the roadside, before the sun rises:
Their lungs are braced for the sharp air of discovery.
The poet must be with these, if his song is to live.
Nothing is beautiful until it has reality,
And art is the apprehension of the real:
Facts are too heavy to hold in the thin tackle of knowledge—
Only the muscles of art can lift them to the light.
The artist is not finer than others—he is stronger.
The battle for a poem is a flesh-tearing maul,
A toe-to-toe, tooth-splintering batter. Stand aside,
Dainty lace-weavers! Go back to lampshades!
Self-conscious ranters, pack up your soap-boxes!
Go and paint picturesque bruises on your foreheads:
'I got this wound, Sir, fighting for Poetry:
Drop a coin in my can! See, how I suffer!
Finance me while I hymn holy poverty!'
The true poet's bruises are inward. His hard bones
Hide in their marrow the ache of his exigence.
His poems can never be cheap, for truth is dear,
And liars of all shapes come to distract him.
There are liars hateful, and liars delightful.
The hateful liars we know: the crazy structure
Of lie on lie, that leans and will one day fall on us;
The fake TV show sponsored by a fake product,
The falsehoods craved by a world dying of falsehood.
But the delightful liars are the poet's sirens:
The lovely soap-bubble grows from the long pipe
Of the grave philosopher with his bottle of questions,
And the theologian round as an Easter bell.
Their structures too are crazy, but how beautiful!

31

Their coloured world spins on an axis of air,
And every day someone gladly accepts that world
For reality, chooses it, trusts his weight to it:
Ping! the bubble vanishes, he is drowned in suds.
Still, to be drowned in suds is not unpleasant;
Mental death by drowning is a sweet relief
From the cliffs and gravel of truthful thinking.
Only the poet with his mouth full of thistles,
Head down and slouching after fugitive truth,
Will nod genially to the delightful liars,
Enjoy their bubble colours in the gay sun—
But never try to pin his songs to a bubble.

X

Still, if the belief-systems are floating bubbles,
Earth-hugging Scepticism offers a mouthful of cork,
A sawdust salad on a paper plate.
Make every poem a cry for belief,
Not belief in a programme, but belief in things,
In solidity, dimension, movement and colour.

The intellectual huckster sets up his stall,
Starts his dynamo, switches his loudspeaker on,
And cries 'Friends, we need belief!'
'Belief in what?' they ask. 'Why, anything!'
He roars with a mechanical smile. 'Believe!
Our age must be an age of faith.' He means:
'Good friends, kindly pin-heads, believe in *me*,
Swallow my recipes for the good life,
Write a blank cheque for my self-esteem.'

I say, too, that we need belief:
Not in programmes, but in things. The booming
Of propaganda cannot make grass less green.
Answer them with the sound of bees among clover
Or the belch of a French navvy full of sausage.
The hinged plate of the lobster defies them,
The smoothness of pebbles is a mocker of slogans.

Believe in the coolness of soil, in the height of a steeple,
In the submissiveness of cities in the hot season:
Believe in the depth of a wave, in the rattle of shingle,
In the important gravity of children,
The gratitude of women for love.
Believe in the shape of a cactus, believe
In the cloud's shadow racing across fields.
Believe in things, and you shall be saved.

So make, I say, your poem a cry for belief,
And never be satisfied with less!
The true poet knows that belief is hard.
The idea-fed man cannot believe in a stone.
He knows the word, and the word destroys his knowledge.
He says 'stone', and the stone disappears
Immediately at the sound of its own name.
The wonder of an elephant is gone
When one says 'elephant', and all our senses
Are blunted and choked with vocabulary's dust,
Pasted over with a dead skin of labels.
But meet the challenge! Strive to believe in air,
In water, in pieces of wood or hairpins!
Struggle to win back your lost perceptions:
Limp on any crutch that comes in handy,
Shamble and trip towards perfection!

W.G.–D   33

Nothing will do for poems but belief:
The poet will be sceptical of programmes,
But credulous of a leaf or an ant-hill.
His credulity is learnt like a hard language:
The grammar is full of quirks and exceptions,
The vocabulary follows no sensible pattern:
But for poems, there is no other language.

XI

And lastly, sing the earth:
but with humility, and shortly. The birds
already do it so much better, at dawn.
They are always awake to the surprise of sunlight.
At evening, circling to their nests,
their cries rock the bounty of the day to rest.
A poet can never compete with the birds:
he must craftily study his own advantage,
his knowledge of time.
               Singing a landscape
contrived by man and nature together,
most painfully shackled, or joyfully hand in hand,
but in any case together, through shadowy centuries,
the poet may hold his ground, even among birds.
For the bird's feet are timeless on the rough bark:
it is always the same blackbird and the same tree,
since these have the magic gift of repetition,
which men, living in time, cannot know.
                      So adapt,
always adapt, adapt or be broken!
Never sing the earth as a bird sings it:
sing the landscape notched with the nails of time,
the fields whorled with the finger-prints of the ages.

A bird sings the moment which lasts for ever,
the explosion which is always happening:
the man sees a tree which grew and will fall,
he sees blossoms break from the deceased bough of winter,
and in their sparkle he glimpses the fires of autumn.
A white road creeps up the medieval hill,
and the sailing bird sees it as a crooked shape;
but the man sees the centuries of peasants,
sacks on their shoulders, heads bent forward,
and the landscape experienced, mostly, as gradient.

This is landscape as the poet can touch it:
supermarket to the bird, gradient to the peasant,
to the tourist a backcloth for his important adventures:
to the poet, the earth:
                    to be sung always,
but modestly, and in songs chiefly short,
and never at dawn, against the voices of birds.

                        XII

So now I close. An end to this crabbed farrago:
The metres limped, but the advice was sound.
It was written in the city which exiled Dante,
And in the spring, which exiles all men from comfort.
Mother of all, look down on your pale poets,
Keep their tongues from brawling and falsehood:
And let truth spin the hub of their syllables!

Wise Men, All Questioning Done

WISE men, all questioning done,
Close up their books and turn to face the sun,
Either that sun of winter, thin and bright
That swerves to earth and brings the early night
Or the full lamp of June, its pounding race half run;

All speculation spent
That rose between the mind and its content,
The quiet brain looks inward at its store
Of chosen objects crammed on shelf and floor,
Knowing them not wisdom's self, but wisdom's instrument.

And there at last
All tribulation stilled, all hazards past,
It sees those intricate bright circles join
That could not chink from hand to hand like coin
But form within a mind that patience has made fast.

Complete, complete,
The old men cry as the last circles meet,
And the clear music of a living tongue
Chimes from the particles it hid among:
For finished work, like answered prayer, makes death taste
    sweet.

Anecdote of 2 a.m.

'WHY was she lost?' my darling said aloud
With never a movement in her sleep. I lay
Awake and watched her breathe, remote and proud.

Her words reached out where I could never be.
She dreamed a world remote from all I was.
'Why was she lost?' She was not asking me.

I knew that there was nothing I could say.
She breathed and dreamed beyond our kisses' sphere.
My watchful night was her unconscious day.

I could not tell what dreams disturbed her heart.
She spoke, and never knew my tongue was tied.
I longed to bless her but she lay apart.

That was our last night, if I could have known.
But I remember still how in the dark
She dreamed her question and we lay alone.

Brooklyn Heights

THIS is the gay cliff of the nineteenth century,
Drenched in the hopeful ozone of a new day.

Erect and brown, like retired sea-captains,
The houses gaze vigorously at the ocean.

With the hospitable eyes of retired captains
They preside over the meeting of sea and river.

On Sunday mornings the citizens revisit their beginnings.
Whose families walk in the fresh air of the past.

Their children tricycle down the nineteenth century:
America comes smiling towards them like a neighbour.

While the past on three wheels unrolls beneath them,
They hammer in the blazing forge of the future.

Brooklyn Bridge flies through the air on feathers.
The children do not know the weight of its girders.

It is the citizens carry the bridge on their shoulders:
Its overhead lights crackle in their blood vessels.

But now it is Sunday morning, and a sky swept clean.
The citizens put down the bridge and stroll at ease.

They jingle the hopeful change in their pockets.
They forget the tripping dance of the profit motive.

The big ships glide in under the high statue,
The towers cluster like spear-grass on the famous island.

And the citizens dream themselves back in a sparkle of morning.
They ride with their children under a sky swept clean.

Dream on, citizens! Dream the true America, the healer,
Drawing the hot blood from throbbing Europe!

Dream the dark-eyed immigrants from the narrow cities:
Dream the iron steamers loaded with prayers and bundles:

Breathe the ozone older than the name of commerce:
Be the citizens of the true survival!

A Song about Major Eatherly

The book (Fernard Gigon's *Formula for Death—The Atom Bombs and After*) also describes how Major Claude R. Eatherly, pilot of the aircraft which carried the second bomb to Nagasaki, later started having nightmares. His wife is quoted as saying: 'He often jumps up in the middle of the night and screams out in an inhuman voice which makes me feel ill: "Release it, release it".'

Major Eatherly began to suffer brief periods of madness, says Gigon. The doctors diagnosed extreme nervous depression, and Eatherly was awarded a pension of 237 dollars a month.

This he appears to have regarded 'as a premium for murder, as a payment for what had been done to the two Japanese cities'. He never touched the money, and took to petty thievery, for which he was committed to Forth Worth prison.

Report in *The Observer*, August 1958.

I

GOOD news. It seems he loved them after all.
His orders were to fry their bones to ash.
He carried up the bomb and let it fall.
And then his orders were to take the cash,

A hero's pension. But he let it lie.
It was in vain to ask him for the cause.
Simply that if he touched it he would die.
He fought his own, and not his country's wars.

His orders told him he was not a man:
An instrument, fine-tempered, clear of stain,
All fears and passions closed up like a fan:
No more volition than his aeroplane.

But now he fought to win his manhood back.
Steep from the sunset of his pain he flew
Against the darkness in that last attack.
It was for love he fought, to make that true.

To take life is always to die a little: to stop
any feeling and moving contrivance, however ugly,
unnecessary, or hateful, is to reduce by so much the total
of life there is. And that is to die a little.

To take the life of an enemy is to help him,
a little, towards destroying your own. Indeed, that is why
we hate our enemies: because they force us to kill them.
A murderer hides the dead man in the ground:
but his crime rears up and topples on to the living,
for it is they who now must hunt the murderer,
murder him, and hide him in the ground: it is they
who now feel the touch of death cold in their bones.

Animals hate death. A trapped fox will gnaw
through his own leg: it is so important to live
that he forgives himself the agony,
consenting, for life's sake, to the desperate teeth
grating through bone and pulp, the gasping yelps.

That is the reason the trapper hates the fox.
You think the trapper doesn't hate the fox?
But he does, and the fox can tell how much.
It is not the fox's teeth that grind his bones,
It is the trapper's. It is the trapper, there,
Who keeps his head down, gnawing, hour after hour.

And the people the trapper works for, they are there too,
heads down beside the trap, gnawing away.
Why shouldn't they hate the fox? Their cheeks are smeared
with his rank blood, and on their tongues his bone
being splintered, feels uncomfortably sharp.

So once Major Eatherly hated the Japanese.

Hell is a furnace, so the wise men taught.
The punishment for sin is to be broiled.
A glowing coal for every sinful thought.

The heat of God's great furnace ate up sin,
Which whispered up in smoke or fell in ash:
So that each hour a new hour could begin.

So fire was holy, though it tortured souls,
The sinners' anguish never ceased, but still
Their sin was burnt from them by shining coals.

Hell fried the criminal but burnt the crime,
Purged where it punished, healed where it destroyed:
It was a stove that warmed the rooms of time.

No man begrudged the flames their appetite.
All were afraid of fire, yet none rebelled.
The wise men taught that hell was just and right.

'The soul desires its necessary dread:
Only among the thorns can patience weave
A bower where the mind can make its bed.'

Even the holy saints whose patient jaws
Chewed bitter rind and hands raised up the dead
Were chestnuts roasted at God's furnace doors.

The wise men passed. The clever men appeared.
They ruled that hell be called a pumpkin face.
They robbed the soul of what it justly feared.

Coal after coal the fires of hell went out.
Their heat no longer warmed the rooms of time,
Which glistened now with fluorescent doubt.

The chilly saints went striding up and down
To warm their blood with useful exercise.
They rolled like conkers through the draughty town.

Those emblematic flames sank down to rest,
But metaphysical fire can not go out:
Men ran from devils they had dispossessed,

And felt within their skulls the dancing heat
No longer stored in God's deep boiler-room.
Fire scorched their temples, frostbite chewed their feet.

That parasitic fire could race and climb
More swiftly than the stately flames of hell.
Its fuel gone, it licked the beams of time.

So time dried out and youngest hearts grew old.
The smoky minutes cracked and broke apart.
The world was roasting but the men were cold.

Now from this pain worse pain was brought to birth,
More hate, more anguish, till at last they cried,
'Release this fire to gnaw the crusty earth:

Make it a flame that's obvious to sight
And let us say we kindled it ourselves,
To split the skulls of men and let in light.

Since death is camped among us, wish him joy,
Invite him to our table and our games.
We cannot judge, but we can still destroy'.

And so the curtains of the mind were drawn.
Men conjured hell a first, a second time:
And Major Eatherly took off at dawn.

IV

Suppose a sea-bird,
its wings stuck down with oil, riding the waves
in no direction, under the storm-clouds, helpless,
lifted for an instant by each moving billow
to scan the meaningless horizon, helpless,
helpless, and the storms coming, and its wings dead,
its bird-nature dead:
                    Imagine this castaway,
loved, perhaps, by the Creator, and yet abandoned,
mocked by the flashing scales of the fish beneath it,
who leap, twist, dive, as free of the wide sea
as formerly the bird of the wide sky,
now helpless, starving, a prisoner of the surface,
unable to dive or rise:
                    this is your emblem.
Take away the bird, let it be drowned
in the steep black waves of the storm, let it be broken
against rocks in the morning light, too faint to swim:
take away the bird, but keep the emblem.

It is the emblem of Major Eatherly,
who looked round quickly from the height of each wave,
but saw no land, only the rim of the sky
into which he was not free to rise, or the silver
gleam of the mocking scales of the fish diving
where he was not free to dive.

Men have clung always to emblems,
to tokens of absolution from their sins.
Once it was the scapegoat driven out, bearing
its load of guilt under the empty sky
until its shape was lost, merged in the scrub.

Now we are civilized, there is no wild heath.
Instead of the nimble scapegoat running out
to be lost under the wild and empty sky,
the load of guilt is packed into prison walls,
and men file inward through the heavy doors.

But now that image, too, is obsolete.
The Major entering prison is no scapegoat.
His penitence will not take away our guilt,
nor sort with any consoling ritual:
this is penitence for its own sake, beautiful,
uncomprehending, inconsolable, unforeseen.
He is not in prison for his penitence:
it is no outrage to our law that he wakes
with cries of pity on his parching lips.
We do not punish him for cries or nightmares.
We punish him for stealing things from stores.

O, give his pension to the storekeeper.
Tell him it is the price of all our souls.
But do not trouble to unlock the door
and bring the Major out into the sun.
Leave him: it is all one: perhaps his nightmares
grow cooler in the twilight of the prison.
Leave him; if he is sleeping, come away.
But lay a folded paper by his head,
nothing official or embossed, a page
torn from your notebook, and the words in pencil.
Say nothing of love, or thanks, or penitence:
say only 'Eatherly, we have your message.'

These poems have appeared in—

AUDIENCE
BULLETIN OF THE ATOMIC SCIENTISTS
COLORADO QUARTERLY
ENCOUNTER
THE LISTENER
THE LONDON MAGAZINE
POETRY (CHICAGO)
THE SPECTATOR
THE TEXAS QUARTERLY

Printed in Great Britain
by W. & J. Mackay & Co Ltd, Chatham

4/8/68